BE A RABBIT EXPERT

Be A Pet Expert

By Gemma Barder

Crabtree Publishing
crabtreebooks.com

BE A RABBIT EXPERT

With their twitchy noses and long, soft ears, it's no wonder rabbits are one of the world's most popular pets. Rabbits are great company and fun to look after, but there are a lot of things you need to know before becoming a real pet expert! In this book you'll discover different breeds of rabbits, where the first pet rabbits came from, and the best way to care for your bunny. When you've finished reading, there's an exciting quiz to reveal if you've really become a pet expert!

Crabtree Publishing

crabtreebooks.com   800-387-7650

Published in 2021 by CRABTREE PUBLISHING COMPANY.

First published in 2019 by Wayland
Copyright © Hodder and Stoughton, 2019

Published in Canada
Crabtree Publishing
616 Welland Avenue
St. Catharines, Ontario
L2M 5V6

Published in the United States
Crabtree Publishing
347 Fifth Avenue
Suite 1402-145
New York, NY 10016

Author: Gemma Barder
Editorial director: Kathy Middleton
Editors: Dynamo Limited, Robin Johnson
Cover and interior design: Dynamo Limited
Proofreader: Melissa Boyce
Production coordinator & prepress technician: Samara
Parent Print coordinator: Katherine Kantor

Printed in Canada/042024/CPC20240415

Library and Archives Canada Cataloguing in Publication
Title: Be a rabbit expert / by Gemma Barder.
Other titles: Rabbits
Names: Barder, Gemma, author.
Description: Series statement: Be a pet expert |
    Previously published under title: Rabbits. | Includes index.
Identifiers: Canadiana (print) 20200222708 |
    Canadiana (ebook) 20200222740 |
    ISBN 9780778780199 (hardcover) |
    ISBN 9780778780472 (softcover) |
    ISBN 9781427125613 (HTML)
Subjects: LCSH: Rabbits—Juvenile literature. |
    LCSH: Rabbit breeds—Juvenile literature.
Classification: LCC SF453.2 .B37 2021 | DDC j636.932/2—dc23

Photographs:
(l - left, br - bottom right, c - center, tr - top right)

All images courtesy of Getty Images iStock except:
Stefan Petru Andronache/Shuttertstock: front cover and title page r;
Denis Tabler/Shutterstock: front cover and title page l; Claudio Contreras/
Naturepl.com: 7b, 29tr; Joy Mennings/Dreamstime.com: 7tr, 30; Michael
Andersen/Alamy: 3tr, 5br; imageBROKER/Alamy: 16; Keren Su/China Span/
Alamy: 18bc; Beryl Peters Collection/Alamy: 19bc; Trinity Mirror / Mirrorpix/
Alamy: 19tr; CuriousCatPhotos/Alamy: 20br

Hardcover   978-0-7787-8019-9
Paperback   978-0-7787-8047-2
Ebook (pdf)   978-1-4271-2561-3

Library of Congress Cataloging-in-Publication Data
Names: Barder, Gemma, author.
Title: Be a rabbit expert / by Gemma Barder.
Description: New York : Crabtree Publishing Company, 2021. |
    Series: Be a pet expert | Includes index.
Identifiers: LCCN 2020015990 (print) |
    LCCN 2020015991 (ebook) |
    ISBN 9780778780199 (hardcover) |
    ISBN 9780778780472 (paperback) |
    ISBN 9781427125613 (ebook)
Subjects: LCSH: Rabbits--Juvenile literature.
Classification: LCC SF453.2 .B365 2021 (print) | LCC SF453.2 (ebook) |
    DDC 632/.6932--dc23
LC record available at https://lccn.loc.gov/2020015990
LC ebook record available at https://lccn.loc.gov/2020015991

CONTENTS

BUNNY BANTER

FIVE FACTS

BUNNY BONANZA

From floppy ears to magnificent markings, get to know these popular bunny **breeds** a bit better.

HOLLAND LOP

This floppy-eared bunny has been popular since the 1950s. With its long ears, beautiful **coat**, and friendly personality, Holland **Lops** make perfect pets. They don't like to be kept cooped up in a **hutch**, though, so make sure you give them plenty of exercise.

DID YOU KNOW?

A rabbit's teeth never stop growing. Rabbits need to nibble and chew almost constantly to keep their teeth short.

MINI REX

The Mini Rex rabbit has a thick coat, straight, soft ears, and a calm personality—which makes it the perfect pet rabbit! Mini Rex rabbits come in many different colors and markings and are slightly smaller than other **domesticated** breeds.

14 million

40 million

There are an estimated 14 million pet rabbits in the world, and scientists believe there could be nearly 40 million in the wild!

JERSEY WOOLY

As their name suggests, these little bunnies have soft coats that feel like wool. They need to be brushed at least once a week. These small rabbits have straight ears and compact bodies. Jersey Woolys are often known as "no-kick bunnies" because they don't usually kick or bite.

DUTCH RABBIT

You can easily spot Dutch rabbits by their distinctive color patterns. Despite their name, they were actually developed in the United Kingdom and were the most popular breed of rabbit for a long time before smaller breeds were introduced. They make smart and playful pets.

DID YOU KNOW?

A female rabbit is called a doe, and a male rabbit is called a buck.

RARE RABBITS

From the smallest to the most mysterious, take a look at these super-rare rabbits.

COLUMBIA BASIN PYGMY RABBIT

These tiny bunnies are the world's smallest breed of rabbit. They weigh only around 1 pound (0.45 kg) when fully grown and are about the same size as a kitten! In the wild, they live in a small area of Washington state and were almost **extinct** in the 1990s.

DID YOU KNOW?

A species called the Sumatran striped rabbit is so rare it has been photographed only a few times!

SOUTHEAST ASIAN STRIPED RABBIT

This unusual rabbit was discovered 20 years ago in the remote Annamite Mountains of Laos and Vietnam, and sightings have been rare ever since. Its fur is light brown with dark-brown stripes. It has short ears and can grow to around 16 inches (40 cm) long. But there is still much more to learn about this mysterious bunny!

TEDDYWIDDER

Is that a rabbit or a big pom-pom? Teddywidders come from the Netherlands, Germany, and Belgium and have fur that grows more than 2 inches (5 cm) long. Teddywidders have floppy (or lop) ears, which makes them slightly different than their Teddy Dwerg cousins that have pointy ears.

DID YOU KNOW?

The volcano rabbit lets out a high-pitched squeak when it thinks it is in danger, rather than thumping its feet on the ground like other breeds do.

VOLCANO RABBIT

Volcano rabbits live in mountainous areas of Mexico. They are very hard to spot and in some areas have been declared extinct. The destruction of their natural habitat, together with **climate change**, has forced this bunny breed to make its home higher up the mountains. Volcano rabbits are the second-smallest rabbit breed in the world and have short, fluffy ears.

BUNNY BANTER

Rabbits have a secret language to tell you (and other rabbits) how they are feeling. Find out exactly what it means when your bunny hops, thumps, and twitches.

EARS

Different rabbit breeds have different types of ears (straight, floppy, small), so it can be hard to tell what they are doing with them. A little shake of the ears followed by jumping shows playfulness and excitement. Ears perked up mean rabbits are feeling cautious about what is going on around them.

□ STANDING

If your rabbit is standing on its hind legs, it could be trying to get a better view of something—or just begging for more food! If it is standing on all fours, it is waiting to see what's next.

NOSE □

Rabbits use their noses as a way of communicating how they feel. Frantic twitching can show they are excited or **anxious**. Nose rubbing is a sign of affection, while nose bumping can mean they want attention—or for you to move out of the way!

LEGS □

One of the most common things rabbits do with their back legs is thump them on the ground. In most cases this means they are scared or unhappy about something. If your rabbit is lying with its legs in the air or flat out behind it, you have one happy bunny!

KITTENS

These cute little bundles don't take long to grow up! Read all about baby bunnies—called kittens—before they hop away!

EARLY DAYS

Kittens are blind and furless when they are born. They live snuggled up to their brothers and sisters in fur-lined nests until they can see and their fur grows. Unlike birds, mother rabbits don't sit on their nests and will leave the kittens for long periods of time.

DID YOU KNOW?

The average number of kittens in a litter is eight to nine. The world record for kittens in one litter is 24!

TIME TO GROW

A baby rabbit should stay with its mother until it is at least eight weeks old. Kittens become adult rabbits when they are around six months old, which is when they can start to have kittens of their own.

30 days

660 days

Rabbits are pregnant for only 30 days, while elephants can be pregnant for 660 days!

WEANING

Newborn kittens drink only their mother's milk. After two weeks, they start to eat other foods such as hay and carrots, before moving on to a variety of other foods.

BUNNY LOVE!

Discover everything you need to know about keeping your bunny happy, healthy, and well fed!

GROOMING

Rabbits like to keep themselves clean, but that doesn't mean you can leave them to look after themselves completely. Long-haired rabbits need to be brushed at least once a week to keep their fur from **matting**, and all rabbits need their nails trimmed regularly.

FOOD AND DRINK

Rabbits need a supply of fresh hay at all times. Bunnies like to **graze** rather than eating a lot of food at once, so snacking between meals is definitely OK! They like fresh vegetables and rabbit pellets, which give them plenty of fiber. They also need fresh water throughout the day in a bowl or bottle.

FUN WITH FRIENDS

A happy rabbit is a rabbit with friends. Rabbits need to be kept with at least one other bunny, and they like to see you too! Spend time with your rabbit at least twice a day.

HEATSTROKE

If your bunny is outside on a hot day, watch for signs of **heatstroke**, which include red ears, drooling, moving slowly, and sometimes **convulsions**.

BUNNY PROOFING

If you are planning to exercise your rabbit indoors, you'll need to do some bunny proofing first! Make sure all wires are tied up out of reach or covered in plastic tubes. Put plastic guards on your baseboards too.

HEALTH

Bunnies can get sick, so it is a good idea to keep an eye on how they behave. If your rabbit is eating less or having trouble pooping, it could be a sign of illness. Watch for an extra-scratchy bunny because it could have fleas!

PLAYTIME

When you play with your rabbit, come down to its level and play on the floor because rabbits don't like to be high up. Make a castle out of old cardboard boxes for your rabbit to explore and chew.

DID YOU KNOW?

Rabbits and guinea pigs do not get along! They don't understand each other and can get into fights.

FACT FILE

TOYS!

Rabbits love to play with toys like these:

■ cardboard tubes stuffed with hay
■ baby toys (not electronic)
■ tunnels

RABBIT RULES

Here are some tips on the dos and don'ts of bunny care.

DO:

Keep rabbits in pairs or in threes because they love company. ✔

Provide two bowls or bottles of water if you are away for more than a few hours. ✔

Buy good-quality food and hay. ✔

Get your bunnies vaccinated. **Your** vet **will tell you which vaccinations they need.** ✔

Research the right type of rabbit for you. ✔

Brush your bunnies regularly. ✔

Keep vegetable peelings to add to their diet. ✔

Play with them often. ✔

DON'T:

Don't keep your rabbits in a hutch or run that is too small. **X**

Don't keep them outside when it is very cold. **X**

Don't pet or play with your bunnies when they are anxious. Leave them alone to calm down. **X**

Don't keep them in a cage with a wire floor because it is bad for their feet. **X**

Don't give them toys they could get stuck in, such as a hamster ball. **X**

Don't forget to clean out their hutch regularly. **X**

FOOD FOR RABBITS

✔		✘	
basil	celery	apple seeds	chocolate
bok choy	clover	avocado	fried food
carrot tops	coriander	bread	onion

RABBIT HABITAT

There's a lot to consider when you begin to create the perfect palace for your rabbit friends. Get started by reading these hints and tips.

INDOORS OR OUTDOORS?

It can be confusing to decide whether your rabbits should live indoors or outdoors. Before you bring your bunnies home, talk to the breeder to see how they have been living. Also consider talking to your vet. Always remember to bring your rabbits indoors if the weather is very cold or hot.

FACT FILE

The Be a Pet Expert guide to hutch size:

■ It should be tall enough for your adult-sized bunny to sit up straight on its back legs.

■ It should be wide enough for your adult-sized bunny to hop twice.

■ It should be long enough for your adult-sized bunny to hop three times.

■ Attach a run to your hutch so your bunny gets plenty of exercise.

HAPPIEST HUTCH

A hutch should have a place for sleeping and a place for looking out. Most hutches have a dark area as well as a section covered in mesh or wire for your bunny to look through.

GETTING READY

Before you introduce your rabbit to its new home, it's time to make it nice and cozy! Start by lining the bottom of the cage with newspaper, then top that with wood shavings (but not cedar or pine because these can be **toxic**). Line the sleeping area of the hutch with soft hay too.

FACT FILE

Where to place your outdoor hutch:
- **Choose a spot that is close to the house.**
- **A shady spot is a great choice for warmer weather.**
- **Be aware of any plants that might hang over the hutch and make sure they aren't toxic to hungry bunnies.**
- **Make sure the hutch is away from other animals.**

THE HISTORY OF RABBITS

From the Spanish wilderness to your backyard, bunnies have a very interesting history.

ROMANS

The ancient Romans knew how important rabbits were for providing food to eat and warm clothing to wear. Although the Romans built rabbit farms, the rabbits were famous for tunneling to freedom.

300 B.C.E.　　　**220 B.C.E.**　　　**40 C.E.**

LAND OF THE RABBITS!

One theory about how Spain got its name dates back to around 2,300 years ago. The theory goes that the ancient Romans called it "Hispania," a word that came from another ancient language and means "Land of the Rabbits."

ACROSS THE OCEANS

As the ancient Romans traveled across the globe, so did their rabbits! Romans would take the rabbits on voyages for food and breed them in each new country they settled in. Many rabbits escaped and found new homes in the fields and countryside.

TODAY

Rabbits are the third-most-popular pet in the world after cats and dogs. There are now more than 200 breeds worldwide.

VICTORIANS

Life changed for some rabbits in the 1800s. The Victorians could see rabbits had other charms besides being hunted and kept for food. It became fashionable to attend rabbit competitions, where owners would compete to see who had the best bunny. People also began to keep rabbits as pets for lucky boys and girls.

600 C.E.   1800s   1939

MONKS

From 600 C.E., there are records of rabbits being kept in **monasteries**, where monks lived and worked. Although the rabbits were still used for food and clothing, the monks took pride in caring for them and began to breed varieties with different coats and markings.

WORLD WAR II

During World War II (1939–1945), the British government encouraged people to keep rabbits to help feed families when food was limited. After the war ended, many people kept their rabbits as pets.

BUNNY STARS

There have been some legendary rabbits in books and on screen. How much do you know about these bunny superstars?

BUGS BUNNY

Everyone has heard of Bugs Bunny. The wisecracking rabbit has been around for nearly 90 years and has his own star on the Hollywood Walk of Fame. His first appearance was in a short cartoon that was nominated for an Oscar!

DID YOU KNOW?

Mel Blanc (the voice of Bugs Bunny) munched on real carrots while recording the character.

PETER RABBIT

When Beatrix Potter first wrote *The Tale of Peter Rabbit*, her publishers didn't think it would be much of a success. Today, the little book has sold more than 40 million copies and has been translated into more than 35 different languages! It has also been turned into a TV series and a popular movie.

THE WHITE RABBIT

If it weren't for this little bunny, Alice may never have fallen down the rabbit hole into Wonderland! Written in 1865 by Lewis Carroll, the book *Alice's Adventures in Wonderland* has made the White Rabbit almost as famous as the Mad Hatter or Alice herself.

DID YOU KNOW?

Alice's Adventures in Wonderland has been translated into 174 different languages!

MIFFY

This cute little white rabbit was created by Dutch artist Dick Bruna in the 1950s and is still popular today. Miffy has been featured in more than 30 books that have sold 85 million copies all over the world. She can be found on everything from pajamas to lunch boxes.

DID YOU KNOW?

Miffy's birthday is June 21 and she is more than 60 years old!

REMARKABLE RABBITS

These rabbits are the biggest, longest, and furriest bunnies around. Keep reading to discover their amazing achievements!

Nipper's Geronimo was an English Lop just like this one!

LONGEST EARS
An English Lop named Nipper's Geronimo had the longest ears of any rabbit. They measured 31 inches (79 cm) long!

OLD-TIMER
The oldest known rabbit lived to be 18 years and 10 months old. He was a wild rabbit caught in Tasmania, Australia, in 1964 and was named Flopsy.

GIANT BUNNY

Darius is a Flemish Giant rabbit, just like the one shown below. At 51 inches (129 cm), he has been recognized as the world's longest rabbit and is about the same size as a small dog. Although they look hard to handle, Flemish Giants are easy to look after because they are so relaxed!

MORE AMAZING BUNNY FACTS!

■ The longest recorded rabbit jump was made by Yabo, a rabbit from Denmark. Yabo's jump measured 9.84 feet (3 m) in length.

■ The highest rabbit jump ever recorded is 39.2 inches (99.5 cm) by a bunny named Mimrelunds Tosen, also from Denmark.

HAIR-RAISING RABBIT

Franchesca is a beautiful English Angora rabbit with record-breaking fur! At 14.37 inches (36.5 cm) long, it is the longest rabbit fur in the world, and Franchesca is often mistaken for a Pekingese dog!

Angora rabbits like this one need to be brushed regularly or their fur can get matted.

DID YOU KNOW?

Angora rabbits can make great pets. They are intelligent and love to play with their owners.

FIVE FACTS

Take a look at these amazing (and sometimes gross) facts about our wonderful bunny friends.

1 THEY EAT THEIR OWN POOP

It's weird, but true! Rabbits make two types of poop: soft black balls and hard pellets. By eating the soft poop, rabbits can get even more **nutrients** from their food.

2 THEY SLEEP WITH THEIR EYES OPEN

Rabbits can fall asleep while they are still on the lookout for predators.

3 THEY AREN'T RODENTS

Rabbits come from a family that also includes hares.

4 THEY CAN'T VOMIT

Rabbits don't have the ability to throw up, so it's vital that you feed them the right food to keep their stomachs healthy.

5 THEY ARE CREPUSCULAR

That is just a fancy way of saying rabbits are most active in the early morning and early evening.

YOUR BEST BUNNY

Can you match your personality to your dream pet?
Answer the questions and follow the arrows to find out!

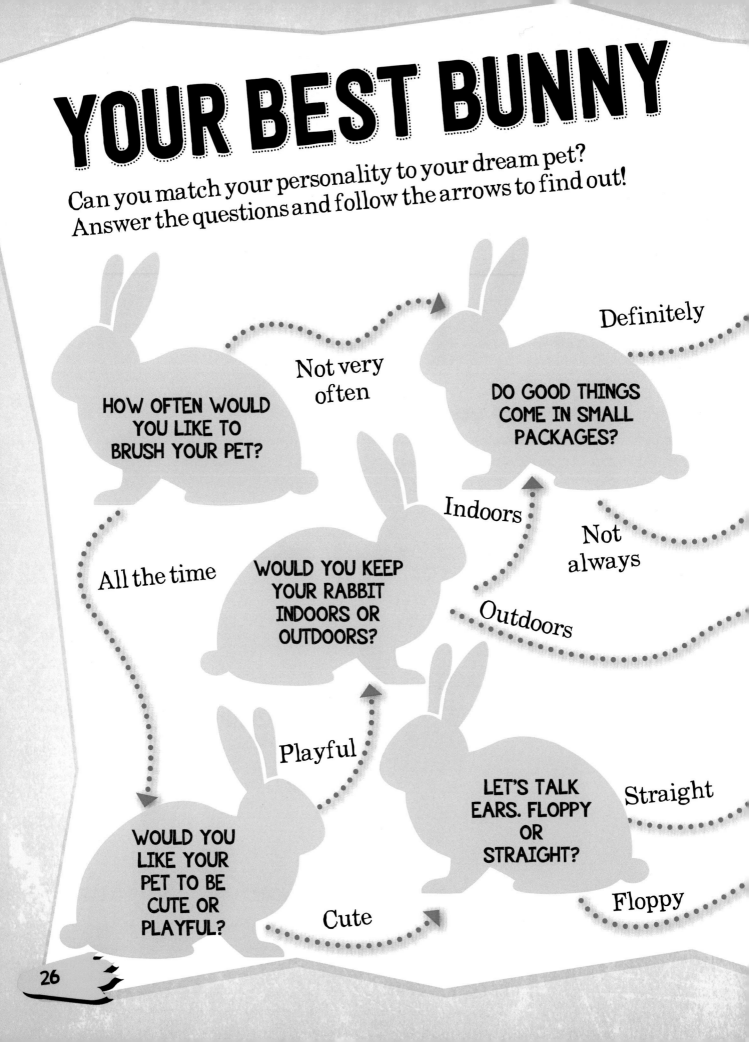

Not very often

HOW OFTEN WOULD YOU LIKE TO BRUSH YOUR PET?

All the time

WOULD YOU KEEP YOUR RABBIT INDOORS OR OUTDOORS?

Indoors

Outdoors

DO GOOD THINGS COME IN SMALL PACKAGES?

Definitely

Not always

Playful

WOULD YOU LIKE YOUR PET TO BE CUTE OR PLAYFUL?

Cute

LET'S TALK EARS. FLOPPY OR STRAIGHT?

Straight

Floppy

WOULD YOUR PET BE BETTER AT SNUGGLING OR HOPPING?

Snuggling

Hopping

WHICH BUNNY DO YOU PREFER— PETER RABBIT OR THUMPER?

Thumper

Peter

MINI REX

The Mini Rex is a cute little bundle that likes a lot of attention. You and your bunny would be best friends and have so much fun together.

DUTCH RABBIT

Dutch rabbits are playful and happy bunnies, which is a great match for you! Give your bunny plenty of toys and attention and you'll be friends forever.

ARE YOU SPORTY?

Yes

No

DO YOU HAVE MANY OTHER PETS?

Yes

No

HOLLAND LOP

If you don't mind a bit of brushing, the Holland Lop is your perfect match. With floppy ears and a stylish hairdo, this is the right rabbit for you!

QUIZ!

Now that you've read all about rabbits, do you think you are a pet expert? Take this quiz to find out!

1 WHAT IS A FEMALE BUNNY CALLED?

a) a flo
b) a doe
c) a bow

2 HOW BIG IS A FULLY GROWN COLUMBIA BASIN PYGMY RABBIT?

a) the same size as a kitten
b) the same size as a fox
c) the same size as a mouse

3 HOW MANY TYPES OF POOP DO RABBITS MAKE?

a) one
b) two
c) three

4 HOW LONG ARE RABBITS PREGNANT FOR?

a) 30 days
b) 60 days
c) 90 days

The answers can be found on page 30.

5 WHY SHOULDN'T YOU KEEP RABBITS AND GUINEA PIGS IN THE SAME HOME?

a) they fight
b) they don't understand each other
c) both of the above

6 WHICH FOOD SHOULD RABBITS AVOID?

a) celery
b) clover
c) avocado

7 WHAT TYPE OF FLOOR IS HARMFUL TO BUNNIES?

a) marble
b) wire
c) wood

8 APPROXIMATELY HOW MANY BREEDS OF RABBITS ARE THERE WORLDWIDE?

a) 20
b) 200
c) 2000

9 WHO WROTE *THE TALE OF PETER RABBIT*?

a) J.K. Rowling
b) Eric Carle
c) Beatrix Potter

10 WHAT TYPE OF RABBIT HAS THE LONGEST FUR?

a) Flemish Giant
b) Dutch rabbit
c) Angora

GLOSSARY

anxious
Worried or nervous

breed
A group of animals that share the same characteristics and physical appearance

climate change
Earth becoming warmer as a result of pollution in the air, which has an effect on the environment

coat
An animal's fur

convulsions
A shaking movement of the body that cannot be controlled

domesticated
Living or working alongside humans

extinct
Describing an animal or plant that no longer exists

graze
To eat lightly throughout the day

heatstroke
An illness caused by being exposed to too much heat

hutch
A rabbit's home, usually made out of wood

lop
Drooping down instead of standing up straight

matting
Tangling into a thick lump

monasteries
Buildings kept for prayer, where monks or nuns live and work

nutrient
A natural substance that helps animals and plants grow

pregnant
Describing a rabbit with kittens growing inside her

run
An outdoor enclosure for a rabbit

toxic
Poisonous

vaccinate
To give medicine to a person or animal to stop them from becoming sick

vet
A medical doctor who treats animals; short for veterinarian

wean
To introduce food other than mother's milk to a baby rabbit

INDEX

Crabtree Publishing
crabtreebooks.com

By Gemma Barder

BE A HORSE AND PONY EXPERT

Be A
Pet Expert

BE A HORSE AND PONY EXPERT

If you love horses and ponies then you have picked up the right book! The following pages are packed with essential information, from how to look after your pony to the history of how horses have helped humans for thousands of years. Horses and ponies are wonderful creatures, but did you know just how amazing they really are? In this book you'll learn about prize ponies and record-breaking horses and find some fascinating horsey facts.

Crabtree Publishing

crabtreebooks.com   800-387-7650

Published in 2021 by CRABTREE PUBLISHING COMPANY.

First published in 2019 by Wayland
Copyright © Hodder and Stoughton, 2019

Published in Canada
Crabtree Publishing
616 Welland Avenue
St. Catharines, Ontario
L2M 5V6

Published in the United States
Crabtree Publishing
347 Fifth Avenue
Suite 1402-145
New York, NY 10016

Author: Gemma Barder
Editorial director: Kathy Middleton
Editors: Dynamo Limited, Robin Johnson
Cover and interior design: Dynamo Limited
Proofreader: Melissa Boyce
Production coordinator & prepress technician: Samara Parent
Print coordinator: Katherine Kantor

Printed in Canada/042024/CPC20240415

Library and Archives Canada Cataloguing in Publication Title:
Be a horse and pony expert / by Gemma Barder.
Other titles: Horses & ponies
Names: Barder, Gemma, author.
Description: Series statement: Be a pet expert |
    Previously published under title: Horses & ponies. | Includes index.
Identifiers: Canadiana (print) 20200222643 |
    Canadiana (ebook) 2020022266X |
    ISBN 9780778780182 (hardcover) |
    ISBN 9780778780465 (softcover) |
    ISBN 9781427125606 (HTML)
Subjects: LCSH: Horses—Juvenile literature. | LCSH: Ponies—
    Juvenile literature. | LCSH: Horse breeds—Juvenile literature.
Classification: LCC SF302 .B37 2021 | DDC j636.1—dc23

Photographs:
(l - left, br - bottom right, c - center, tr - top right)

Bob Langrish/Alamy: 3tr, 6cr; Joel Sartore/National Geographic/Alamy: 6bl, 29br; Juniors Bildarchiv GmbH/Alamy: 7t; Betty Shelton/Shutterstock: 11t; JFJacobsz/Shutterstock: 12tl; Charles Walker Collection/Alamy: 19tr; Everett - Art/Shutterstock: 19bc; The Picture Art Collection/Alamy: 20bl; Geraint Lewis/Alamy: 21br; M & N/Alamy: 23tr

Every attempt has been made to clear copyright. Should there be any inadvertent omission, please apply to the publisher for rectification.

Hardcover	978-0-7787-8018-2
Paperback	978-0-7787-8046-5
Ebook (pdf)	978-1-4271-2560-6

Library of Congress Cataloging-in-Publication Data
Names: Barder, Gemma, author.
Title: Be a horse and pony expert / by Gemma Barder.
Description: New York : Crabtree Publishing Company, 2021. |
    Series: Be a pet expert | Includes index.
Identifiers: LCCN 2020015992 (print) |
    LCCN 2020015993 (ebook) |
    ISBN 9780778780182 (hardcover) |
    ISBN 9780778780465 (paperback) |
    ISBN 9781427125606 (ebook)
Subjects: LCSH: Horses--Juvenile literature. | Ponies--Juvenile literature.
Classification: LCC SF302 .B365 2021 (print) | LCC SF302 (ebook) |
    DDC 636.1--dc23
LC record available at https://lccn.loc.gov/2020015992
LC ebook record available at https://lccn.loc.gov/2020015993

CONTENTS

HARD-TO-FIND HORSES

HELPFUL HINTS

HORSE-KEEPING

FOALS

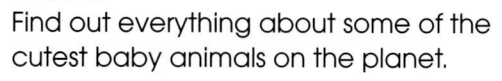

HUNDREDS OF HORSES

Horses and ponies come in different shapes and sizes, each with its own unique personality. Find out the differences between our equine friends.

WHICH IS IT?

It can be tricky to tell the difference between a horse and pony. Usually ponies are shorter than horses. Any adult equine shorter than 14.2 **hands** is probably a pony, but there are exceptions to the rule, such as miniature horses.

Horses and ponies are both part of the equine family, but they are different animals.

DID YOU KNOW?
The unit used to measure horses and ponies is called a hand, which is about **4** inches (10 cm). A horse's height is measured from the top of its withers (shoulder blades) to the ground.

HORSES VS. PONIES

Horses and ponies are different in many ways:

- For their size, ponies are stronger than horses.
- Horses are faster than ponies.
- Ponies are generally considered smarter than horses.
- Horses grow slower than ponies.
- Ponies tend to have thicker **manes** and coats than horses.
- Horses need a lot more food than ponies.
- Ponies live longer than horses.

HORSE OR PONY

See if you can tell the difference between a pony and a horse the next time you pass a **paddock** or go to a **stable**.

SHIRE HORSE

Shires are gentle giants. Their average height is 17 hands (68 inches or 173 cm), but they can grow much larger. You can spot a Shire by its shaggy **hooves** and muscular frame, which is perfect for heavy work such as pulling tree trunks and plows. These calm horses don't get spooked easily.

THOROUGHBRED

Thoroughbreds have long legs, sleek coats, and lean bodies, which makes them perfect for horse racing, polo, and other high-speed sports. They are called "hot-blooded" because of their strong and spirited nature and can grow to around 16 hands (64 inches or 163 cm). They are also expensive— young racehorses are sold for millions of dollars.

SHETLAND PONY

Shetland ponies grow to around 8 hands (32 inches or 81 cm) and can pull up to twice their own weight! Their small, powerful frames meant they were once sent to work in cramped coal mines in Britain and the United States. Today, Shetland ponies are ideal for small children to ride.

HARD-TO-FIND HORSES

There are hundreds of **breeds** of horses and ponies in the world. Keep reading to discover some you might not have heard of!

Caspian horses are are a great choice for show jumping!

AMERICAN CREAM

This is a **draft horse**, which means it is big and strong like a Shire. The color of its coat is called gold champagne, which is a mixture of the colors champagne and chestnut. American Creams have amazing eyes—they are almost white at birth, then turn to a dark orange-yellow color.

CASPIAN

Caspians are one of the most ancient breeds of horses still around today. Scientists believed these horses were **extinct** until they were rediscovered in Iran in 1965. Although Caspians are small compared to other horses, they are still considered horses because of the way they look.

There are just 250 American Creams left in the world today.

HACKNEY

Admired for their unique high **trot** and majestic features, Hackney horses were a popular breed for pulling carriages in the late 1800s. When people began to swap their carriages for cars, the Hackney lost its appeal and in 2012 it was added to the list of **critically endangered** species.

FACT FILE

STUNNING: AKHAL-TEKE

This golden-colored horse originally came from Turkmenistan and is the national symbol of that country. It forms a really strong bond with whoever rides it first and doesn't like to change owners.

GRACEFUL: LIPIZZAN

For centuries, this beautiful horse has been bred for **dressage**—a kind of riding where the horse and rider perform a series of special movements. Although adult Lipizzans are gray, they are born black or brown.

60 million

350

There are about 60 million horses on the planet, and there are more than 350 different breeds of horses.

DID YOU KNOW?

In the horse world, white horses are always called grays.

7

BODY LANGUAGE

Horses and ponies give us many clues to how they are feeling. All you have to do is look carefully and read the signs.

THE BIG PICTURE □ - - - -

Take a step back and look at your horse to see how it is feeling. If its muscles are tensed and its movements are stiff, your horse could be nervous, stressed, or in pain.

TAIL □ - - - - - - - - - - -

A raised tail can indicate your horse is excited and ready for fun. If a horse's tail is clamped down against its bottom, it usually means the horse is upset or **anxious** about something. A swishing tail shows that a horse is irritated.

Horses can sleep standing up, so be careful when greeting a horse with its eyes closed. It could be having a quick snooze!

BACK LEGS □ - -

Stepping behind the powerful back legs of a horse can be dangerous, so make sure you keep clear at all times—even if you think your horse is calm. If one leg is lifted, your horse is showing you it is upset or spooked.

EARS

If a horse's ears are perked up it means the horse is alert and happy. However, if the ears are turned out to the side it could be a sign that the horse is sleepy. If the ears are flicking forward and backward or are pinned back toward the horse's neck, your horse may be feeling anxious.

DID YOU KNOW?

Horses and ponies can see most of what is around them at all times because of the position of their eyes on either side of their heads.

EYES

Most of the time, you can see only the pupil and the colored part of a horse's eye. If you start to see the white part of a horse's eyes, it can be a sign the horse is scared or upset.

HEAD

A horse that holds its head up is alert and aware of everything around it. If the head is lowered, it's a sign your horse is relaxing—or it could even be asleep! A horse that swishes its head and neck from side to side like a snake could be feeling aggressive, so be very careful around it.

FRONT LEGS

When a horse is digging with one of its front hooves, that usually means it wants something. The horse may also stamp its front legs from time to time to show frustration or anger.

FOALS

We all know baby horses and ponies are very cute, but did you know they also develop really quickly and learn a lot in just their first year? Keep reading to discover more!

FIRST STEPS

Foals can stand up and take their first steps just two hours after they are born. It can take human babies about a year to do this!

Have you ever noticed how long a foal's legs are? That's because they are almost the same length they will be when the horse is fully grown.

FOOD FOR FOALS

Milk from its mother gives a young foal everything it needs for the first three months of its life, but it can also start eating grass at six weeks.

Foals and their mothers bond very quickly and stay together for at least six months until the foals are weaned.

DID YOU KNOW?

Foals begin to develop teeth during the first week of life. (Adult horses have up to 40 teeth.)

10%   **90%**

A healthy foal should weigh 10 percent of its mother's weight. Within two years, the foal will grow to about 90 percent of its adult size.

SPRING INTO LIFE

It takes 11 months for a foal to grow inside its mother before it is ready to come into the world. Horse breeders like foals to be born in the springtime so the young horses can spend the warm spring and summer months running around outside getting big and strong.

HORSE-KEEPING

Looking after a horse or pony is a lot of fun, but there's also plenty of hard work to be done! To help you prepare, here's a guide to looking after your equine friend.

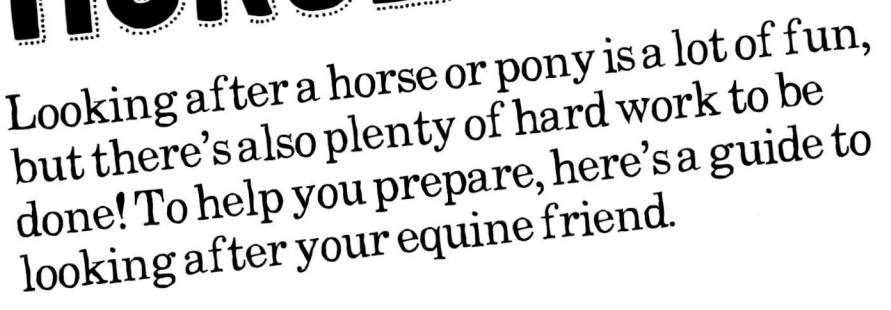

HOOF CARE

Hooves should be inspected each day and cleaned out often, especially after a long ride or job. If your horse or pony gets something lodged in its hoof or if its shoe slips, it can be very uncomfortable and lead to problems in its legs and back.

FOOD AND DRINK

Horses and ponies eat a mixture of **forage** and food such as oats, grains, and pellets. They should be allowed to **graze** on forage as much as they want. Fresh water is also really important, so make sure your horse or pony's **trough** is always clean and full.

HEALTH CHECK

It's very important to check your horse or pony each day and let a **vet** know if you think it is sick. Like many animals, horses and ponies need to be given medicine regularly to help keep them healthy and strong.

DID YOU KNOW?

"Forage" is another word for grass and hay.

DID YOU KNOW?

Horses and ponies need to be taken to **farriers** every six weeks to have their hooves trimmed and their shoes replaced.

MANE ATTRACTION

If your horse or pony's mane is loose (not tied up), you will need to keep it clean and free of tangles. Use a special horse brush to remove dirt from the mane. You can also learn how to braid and knot your equine's mane to keep it tidy and clean.

Make sure you clean your horse's brushes often and don't use them on other horses. Sharing brushes can spread infections.

KEEPING CLEAN

The best way to keep your horse or pony clean is to brush it every day and wash it when needed. Brushing your pet gets rid of dirt and helps you develop trust and friendship with your favorite animal.

TEETH AND GUMS

It's hard to see all of a horse or pony's teeth, but you can still keep an eye on how they are developing. Watch out for any changes or signs of irritation. You should also keep track of how your horse or pony's breath smells! If it gets super-smelly it could be a sign of disease.

DID YOU KNOW?
Horses and ponies should be seen by equine dentists once a year.

13

HELPFUL HINTS

There are a lot of things to remember when looking after a horse or pony. Take a look at these top dos and don'ts.

DO:

Give your horse or pony plenty of exercise. ✔

Make sure it has plenty of outdoor space to roam, and a warm, dry stable. ✔

Brush your horse or pony's coat, mane, and tail every day. ✔

Look at your equine's face for clues to how it is feeling. It can tell you a lot! ✔

Keep the water trough clean and full. Horses and ponies need a lot of water! ✔

Make sure there is plenty of grass and hay to graze on. ✔

Pet your horse or pony's nose to say hello. ✔

Keep your equine with others. They get lonely if they don't have companions. ✔

DON'T:

Don't walk behind a horse or pony. ✕

Don't feed your equine moldy or dusty hay. ✕

Don't ride a horse or pony with poorly fitting tack. ✕

Don't let anyone too big ride a small horse or pony. ✕

Don't forget to check hooves and teeth daily. ✕

Don't leave poisonous plants such as ragwort in the paddock. ✕

✔ FOOD FOR HORSES AND PONIES ✕

✔	✕
apples	chocolate
celery	onions
bananas	garlic
grass	potatoes
carrots	meat
hay	tomatoes

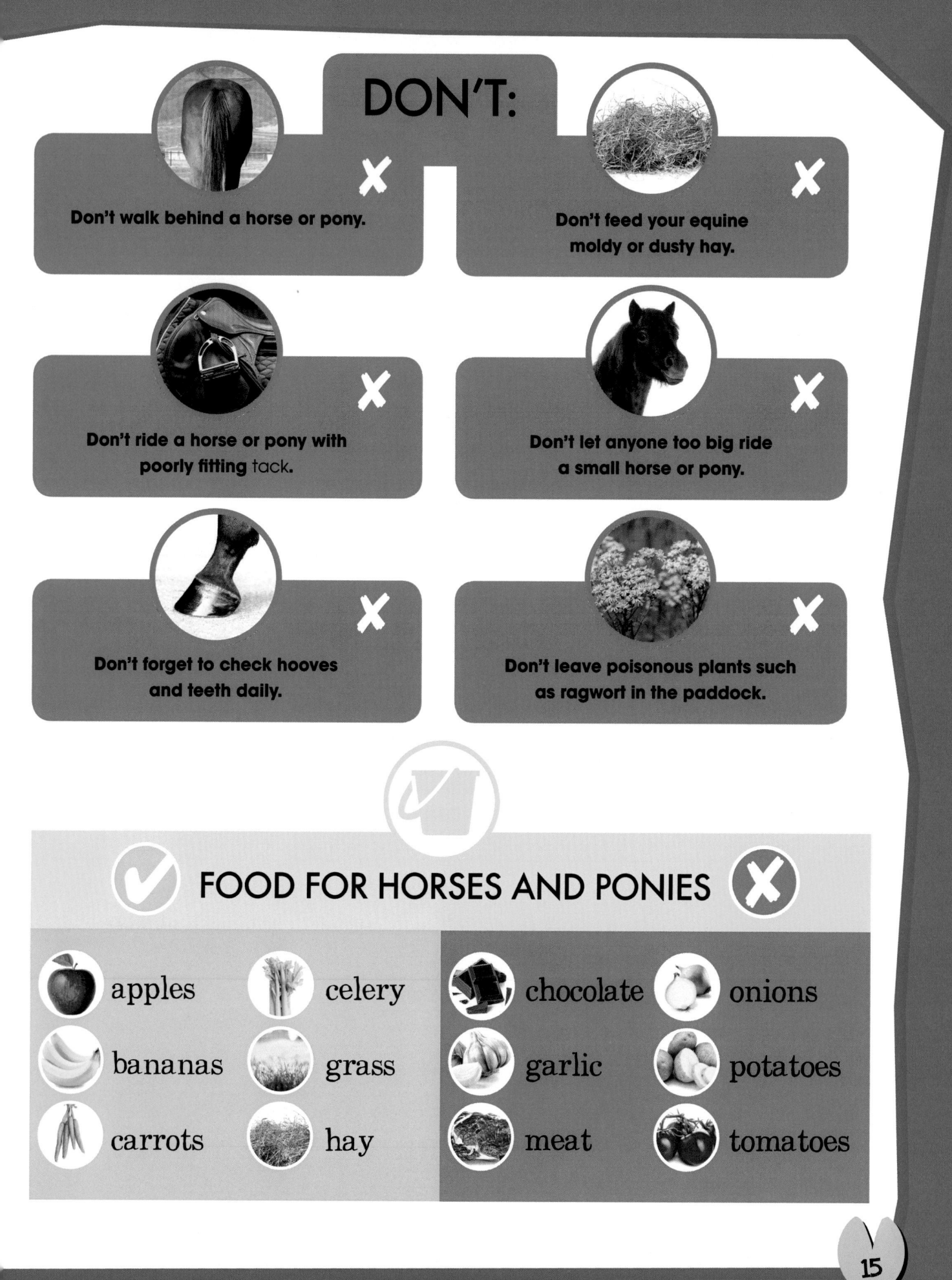

THE PERFECT STABLE

Most of your horse or pony's time should be spent in a large paddock with at least one friend, but it also needs a cozy place to spend time inside. Here are some top tips for making a super stable.

BEDDING

Give your horse somewhere cozy to snuggle up in at night. Horse bedding is traditionally made out of straw, but you can also use special shredded paper, wood chips, or wood pellets.

FOOD AND DRINK

Horses and ponies need a constant supply of water to drink and food to graze on. The stable should have a raised hay net or trough for food and a good supply of water to keep your pet happy until it's time to go outside again.

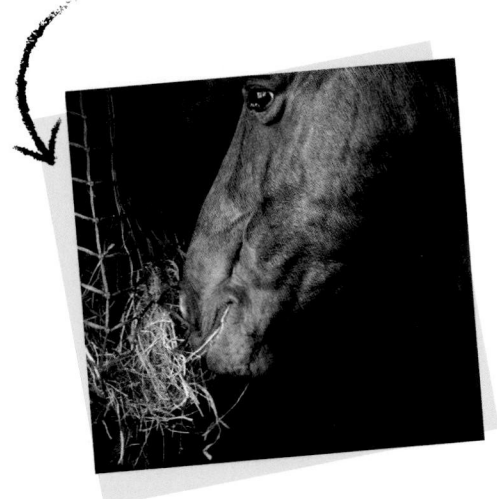

SPACE

A stall should be big enough for your equine to move around in comfortably—at least 12 feet by 12 feet (3.7 m x 3.7 m) for a horse and 9.8 feet by 9.8 feet (3 m x 3 m) for a pony.

MUCKING OUT

Mucking out means cleaning your horse or pony's stable. You will need to clear out any poop and wet bedding each day and replace it with clean, dry bedding for your pet to sleep on.

HELLO THERE!

All stables have doors called Dutch doors that can be closed at the bottom, while the top half stays open. These doors make sure that plenty of fresh air gets into the stable, while letting your curious horse have a look outside whenever it wants.

TROT THROUGH TIME

Horses and ponies have been helping humans for thousands of years. From pulling carriages to fighting in wars, find out how horses and ponies have shaped the world.

PICTURE THAT!

The first drawings showing humans riding horses are 4,000 years old and came from the Middle East. The images show that horses were also used for milk and meat.

4000 B.C.E.

2000 B.C.E.

100 C.E.

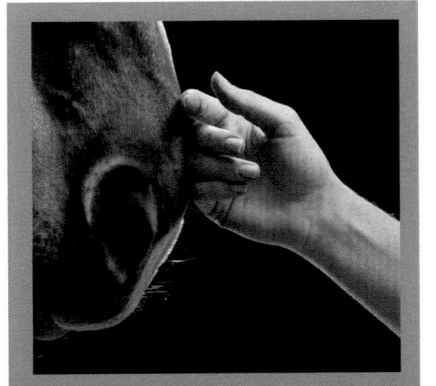

LONG-TERM RELATIONSHIP

The first evidence of horses being tamed to live alongside humans was more than 6,000 years ago. Archaeological evidence from Ukraine in Eastern Europe and Kazakhstan in Central Asia shows large numbers of horses living with humans.

SUPER-FAST HIGHWAY

Once humans figured out they could ride horses, they were able to travel a lot faster and carry more things with them. When horses were hitched to carts, people began buying and selling products, and soon the first roads were invented for horses and carts to travel on.

DID YOU KNOW?

The Uffington White Horse (right) has been visible on the side of a hill in Oxfordshire, England, for more than 3,000 years. Some people believe it is a picture of one of the horses that pulled the Sun across the sky in **Norse** mythology.

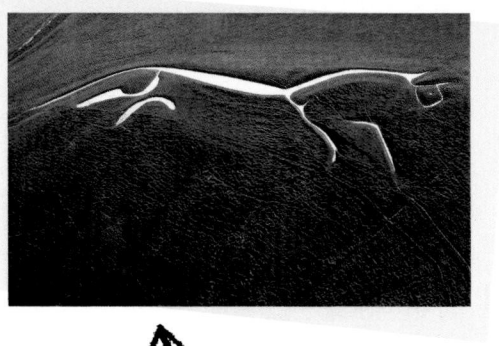

The White Horse is cleaned regularly by a team of volunteers.

TRANSPORTATION TO SPORTS

In 1698, the steam engine was invented and about 100 years later the first steam trains appeared. People began to use horses less for travel and transporting goods and more for sports and leisure. Once cars and trucks hit the roads, horses were no longer used for taking goods from place to place.

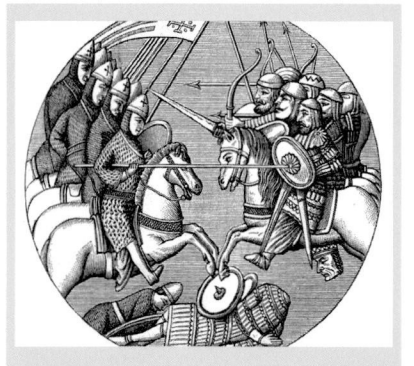

1200s	1800s	2000s

BRED FOR SUCCESS

Horses and ponies were used for many different tasks. Some needed to be strong to work in the fields or fast to deliver messages. Others needed to be brave and tough for the battlefield. That is how many of our modern-day horse and pony breeds came into being.

HORSES TODAY

Horses and ponies are still an important part of life. They are used by the police and the army, and in many different sports such as racing and show jumping. But most importantly, they are still beloved family pets!

FAMOUS FRIENDS

Horses are incredible animals. It's no wonder they are the stars of legendary tales, sports, and best-selling novels worldwide.

BUCEPHALUS

Bucephalus was the legendary horse of Alexander the Great (356–323 B.C.E.), the mighty king who united Greece and conquered the Persian Empire. Everyone thought Bucephalus could not be tamed, so Alexander asked his owner if he could keep the horse if he was able to ride him. Alexander succeeded, and Bucephalus later became known as the bravest horse in history.

ECLIPSE

Eclipse lived from 1764 until 1789 and is one of the most famous racehorses in history. He was undefeated during his racing career and eventually had to stop competing because no one wanted to run against him! All of today's Thoroughbreds can be traced back to this champion horse.

DID YOU KNOW?

Eclipse had a larger-than-average heart, which he passed down to some of his descendants—including a legendary racehorse from the 1970s named Secretariat.

BLACK BEAUTY

Black Beauty is probably the world's most famous book about a horse. It was written in 1877 by Anna Sewell and tells the tale of a beautiful jet-black horse named Black Beauty. It is famous for being one of the first books ever to talk about animal welfare.

WAR HORSE

War Horse tells the story of a farm horse named Joey who is sold to the army, leaving his owner and best friend Albert behind. It was written in 1982 by Michael Morpurgo and has since been made into an award-winning play and a movie directed by Steven Spielberg.

DID YOU KNOW?

There are 23 life-size puppets in the play *War Horse* and puppeteers have to train for eight weeks before going on stage.

EXTRAORDINARY EQUINES

From the highest jump to the smallest horse, these incredible horses have broken records. Discover more about these amazing animals!

SMARTEST HORSE

One very clever Thoroughbred named Lukas set a record for identifying 19 numbers in 60 seconds! Lukas's trainer placed the numbers one through five on a board in front of Lukas. The smart horse then used his nose to point to the correct number after it was called out!

HIGHEST-JUMPING HORSE

The highest jump by a horse was recorded in 1949 in Chile. The horse was named Huaso and he jumped to a huge height of 8.1 feet (2.47 m).

$70 million

$8,000

Fusaichi Pegasus is the world's most expensive racehorse. He was sold for around $70 million in 2000.

Legendary racehorse Seabiscuit was sold for $8,000 in 1936.

Statue of Seabiscuit

FASTEST HORSE

A racehorse named Winning Brew was clocked going 43.97 miles per hour (70.76 kph) at the Penn National Race Course in Pennsylvania in 2008.

TALLEST HORSE

Big Jake is the world's tallest horse. At just over 20 hands (79.9 inches or 203 cm), he is taller than most professional basketball players! He makes use of his large size by helping out on a farm in Michigan. According to his owner, Big Jake is a friendly horse and is loved by all the other farm animals!

Big Jake

Thumbelina

SMALLEST HORSE

The world's smallest equine ever was a miniature horse named Thumbelina. She measured a tiny 17.5 inches (44.5 cm) in height, which meant she was just over 4 hands tall!

FIVE FACTS

Have you ever wondered why your pony never needs to lie down, or what to give it for a special treat? Get ready to discover five things you never knew about horses and ponies!

1 THEY HAVE REALLY BIG EYES

Horses and ponies have the largest eyes of any mammals on land. Their pupils are wide slits and their eyes can see nearly all the way around their bodies. Their eyes developed this way to make sure the animals could see **predators** when they were grazing in the wild!

2 THEY HAVE UNIQUE KNEES

Horses and ponies lock their knees when they sleep. This allows them to sleep standing up without falling over.

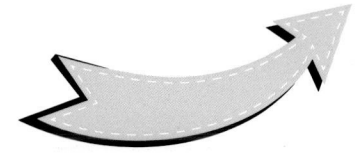

3 THEY ONLY HAVE ONE TOE

Horses and ponies technically only have one toe on each foot—the hoof. Their hooves are made of a substance called keratin, which is the same substance our fingernails are made of.

4 THEIR EARS ARE LIKE THERMOMETERS

You can take a horse's temperature by placing your hand behind its ear. This will give you an idea of how warm or cool the horse's body is.

5 THEY HAVE A SWEET TOOTH

Horses and ponies love sweet treats such as bananas, sugar cubes, and even mints, but these foods should be given only from time to time because they can be bad for their teeth.

YOUR PERFECT PET

Which of these horses and ponies best reflects the type of person you are? Follow the arrows to find out!

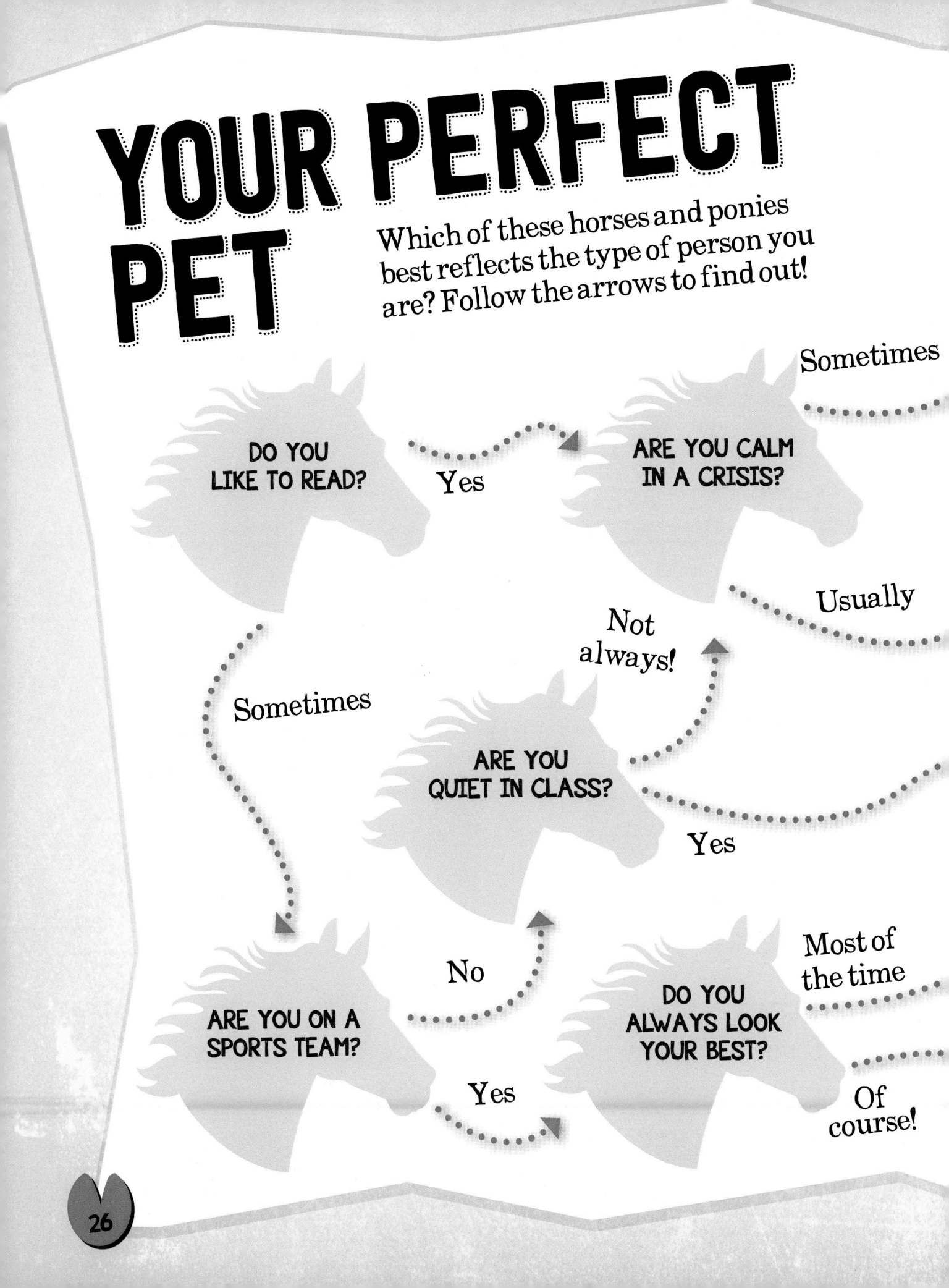

DO YOU LIKE TO READ?

Yes

ARE YOU CALM IN A CRISIS?

Sometimes

Usually

Not always!

ARE YOU QUIET IN CLASS?

Sometimes

Yes

No

ARE YOU ON A SPORTS TEAM?

Yes

DO YOU ALWAYS LOOK YOUR BEST?

Most of the time

Of course!

DO YOU STICK UP FOR YOURSELF? Definitely

Sometimes

SHETLAND PONY
These little ponies may seem sweet, but they are strong and determined. Just like you, they won't let anyone down and love being around people.

DO ALL GOOD THINGS COME IN SMALL PACKAGES? Yes

No

Sometimes

No

SHIRE HORSE
Shire horses are the big, friendly giants of the equine world. They quietly help others and like to observe the world around them.

DO YOU LOVE TO TAKE CHARGE?

Slow

THOROUGHBRED
These swift, sleek horses need a lot of care, attention, and exercise—just like you. You're the perfect match for these energetic equines!

ARE YOU SLOW AND STEADY OR FAST AND FURIOUS? Fast

QUIZ!

Now that you've learned all about horses and ponies, are you a true equine expert? Answer these questions to find out.

1 HANDS ARE USED TO MEASURE HORSES AND PONIES. HOW BIG IS A HAND?

a) 2 inches (5 cm)
b) 4 inches (10 cm)
c) 6 inches (15 cm)

2 HOW MANY AMERICAN CREAM HORSES ARE LEFT IN THE WORLD?

a) 250
b) 2,500
c) 25,000

3 WHAT DO HORSES AND PONIES DO WITH THEIR EARS WHEN THEY ARE ANXIOUS?

a) perk them up
b) let them hang to the side
c) flick them backward and forward

4 HOW LONG DOES IT TAKE FOR A FOAL TO STAND UP AFTER IT IS BORN?

a) two hours
b) two days
c) two weeks

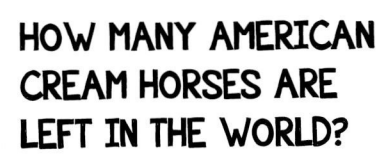

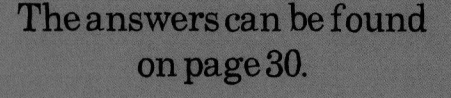

The answers can be found
on page 30.

5 WHY SHOULDN'T YOU USE YOUR HORSE'S BRUSH ON OTHER HORSES?

a) horses get jealous if their brushes are used on others
b) you could spread infection
c) it makes the bristles weak

7 WHAT IS ANOTHER NAME FOR A STABLE DOOR?

a) a French door
b) a Dutch door
c) a German door

6 WHAT IS THE BEST WAY TO SAY HELLO TO YOUR HORSE?

a) a shout and a big wave
b) walk in backward
c) gently pet its nose

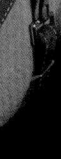

29

8 ROUGHLY HOW MANY HORSES ARE ON THE PLANET?

a) 20 million
b) 40 million
c) 60 million

9 WHO WROTE *BLACK BEAUTY?*

a) Anna Sewell
b) Enid Blyton
c) J.K. Rowling

10 WHAT'S THE NAME OF THE WORLD'S SMALLEST HORSE?

a) Thumbelina
b) Pixie
c) Tiny

QUIZ ANSWERS

1b 2a 3c 4a 5b 6c 7b 8c 9a 10a